THE STANLEY CUP FINALS

BY ALLAN MOREY

BELLWETHER MEDIA · MINNEAPOLIS, MN

TM

Are you ready to take it to the extreme? Torque books thrust you into the action-packed world of sports, vehicles, mystery, and adventure. These books may include dirt, smoke, fire, and chilling tales. **WARNING** : read at your own risk.

This edition first published in 2019 by Bellwether Media, Inc.

Library of Congress Cataloging-in-Publication Data

Names: Morey, Allan, author.
Title: The Stanley Cup Finals / by Allan Morey.
Description: Minneapolis, Minnesota : Bellwether Media, Inc., 2019. | Series: Torque: Sports Championships | Includes bibliographical references and index. | Audience: Ages: 7-12. | Audience: Grades: 3 through 7.
Identifiers: LCCN 2018001782 (print) | LCCN 2018003257 (ebook) | ISBN 9781626178656 (hardcover : alk. paper) | ISBN 9781681036069 (ebook) | ISBN 9781618914859 (paperback : alk. paper)
Subjects: LCSH: Stanley Cup (Hockey)–History–Juvenile literature. | Hockey–History–Juvenile literature.
Classification: LCC GV847.7 (ebook) | LCC GV847.7 .M67 2019 (print) | DDC 796.962/648–dc23
LC record available at https://lccn.loc.gov/2018001782

Editor: Rebecca Sabelko   Designer: Jon Eppard

Printed in the United States of America, North Mankato, MN.

TABLE OF CONTENTS

SHUTOUT GOALIE

It is the 2017 National Hockey **League** (NHL) Stanley Cup Final. The Nashville Predators face the Pittsburgh Penguins. The hard-fought series is tied 2–2.

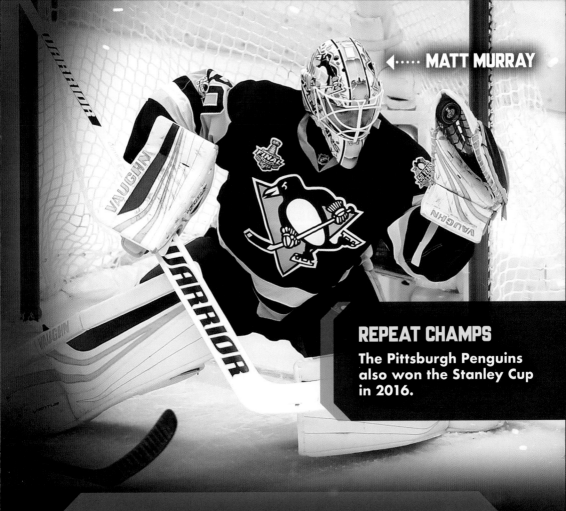

◄····· **MATT MURRAY**

REPEAT CHAMPS

The Pittsburgh Penguins also won the Stanley Cup in 2016.

But things change in Game 5. Penguins **goalie** Matt Murray makes **save** after save. The Predators cannot score, and the Penguins win 6-0. Murray shuts out the Predators in Game 6, too. The Penguins take home the Stanley Cup!

WHAT ARE THE STANLEY CUP FINALS?

The Stanley Cup Finals decide the NHL champion. This series of games is played at the end of every NHL hockey season. The Finals start in the spring.

The Stanley Cup Final is a best-of-seven series. The first team to win four games is the champion. The winning team receives the Stanley Cup trophy.

The Stanley Cup is one of the oldest trophies in **professional** sports. It is also one of the most unique.

The bowl of the trophy sits atop several rings. The names of players from the winning teams are **engraved** on these rings. As more room is needed, the oldest ring is removed and a new ring is added.

STANLEY ·····▶
CUP

RECYCLED TROPHY

Most professional sports leagues make a new trophy each year for the new champion. But in the NHL, the Stanley Cup is passed from one champion to the next.

HISTORY OF THE STANLEY CUP

The Stanley Cup was named after Frederick Stanley. He governed Canada in the late 1800s. He was also a big hockey fan.

FREDERICK STANLEY

1893 MONTREAL AMATEUR ATHLETIC ASSOCIATION TEAM

Stanley purchased a large silver bowl to be awarded to the best **amateur** hockey team in Canada. In 1893, the Montreal Amateur Athletic Association team was the first to win the Stanley Cup.

At first, only amateur teams competed for the Stanley Cup. But in the early 1900s, professional hockey leagues started springing up. Their teams competed for the cup, too.

In 1917, the NHL, a professional league, was founded. A year later, the Toronto Arenas were the first NHL team to win the trophy. Starting in 1926, the Stanley Cup was only awarded to NHL teams.

1926 STANLEY CUP MVP, NELS STEWART

NHL STANLEY CUP CHAMPS

MONTREAL CANADIENS

1924, 1930, 1931, 1944, 1946, 1953, 1956, 1957, 1958, 1959, 1960, 1965, 1966, 1968, 1969, 1971, 1973, 1976, 1977, 1978, 1979, 1986, 1993

STANLEY CUP MVP

Maurice Richard played for the Canadiens from 1942 to 1960. He was the first player to score 50 goals in a season. At the end of his career, he was the league's all-time scoring leader.

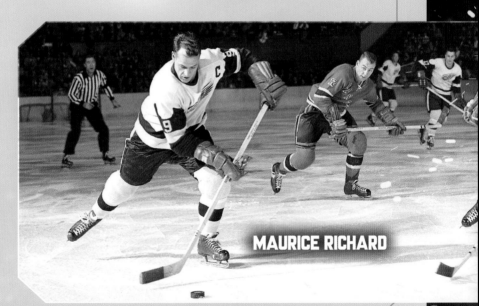

MAURICE RICHARD

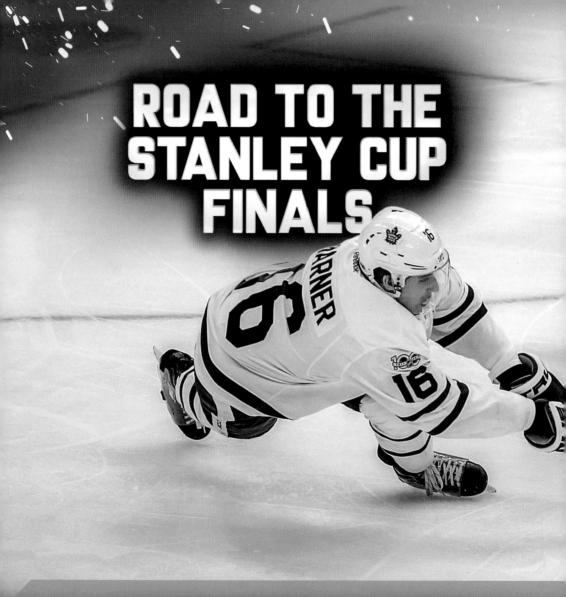

ROAD TO THE STANLEY CUP FINALS

The NHL has two **conferences**. They are the Eastern and the Western Conferences. Each is split into two **divisions**

Each conference has 8 teams that make it to the **playoffs**. The 3 teams with the best records from each division receive spots. There are also 2 **wild card** spots in each conference. These are for the teams with the next best records.

There are four rounds in the playoffs. A best-of-seven-game series decides the winner of each round.

In the first round, 16 teams play. The 8 winners move on to the second round. The 4 winners from the second round move on to the Conference Finals. They determine the 2 teams that play in the Stanley Cup Final.

NHL PLAYOFF BRACKET

WEST
CONFERENCE

FIRST ROUND

SECOND ROUND

CONFERENCE
FINALS

STANLEY CUP
FINAL

NHL CHAMPION

EAST CONFERENCE

STANLEY CUP FINAL

CONFERENCE FINALS

SECOND ROUND

FIRST ROUND

TRAVELING TROPHY

The Stanley Cup is a traveling trophy. Players from the winning team get personal days with it. Players have taken it with them on boats and airplanes. The Stanley Cup has even been to military bases in support of overseas troops.

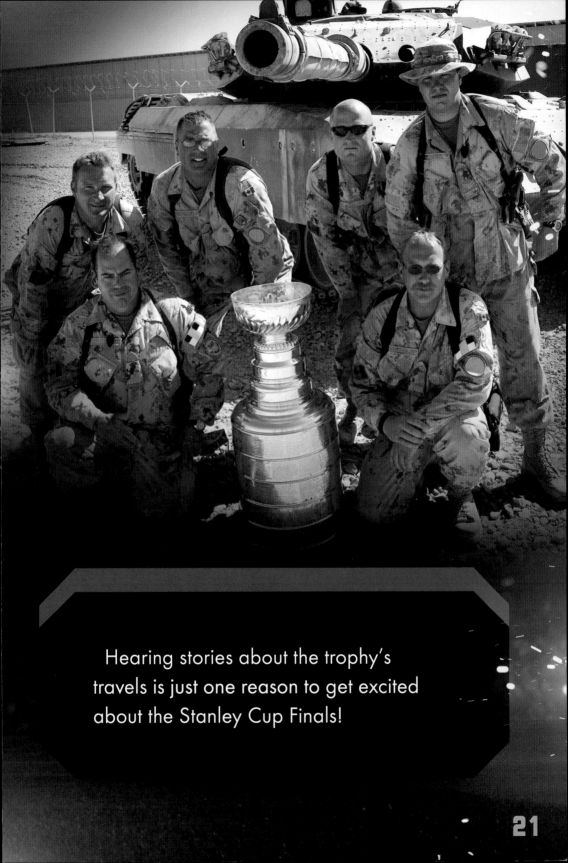

Hearing stories about the trophy's travels is just one reason to get excited about the Stanley Cup Finals!

GLOSSARY

amateur—relating to a player or team that plays a sport without payment

conferences—large groupings of sports teams that often play each other

divisions—small groupings of sports teams; there are usually several divisions of teams in a conference.

engraved—cut or carved into

goalie—a defensive player who defends the goal

league—a large group of sports teams that often play each other

playoffs—games played after the regular season is over; playoff games determine which teams play in the Stanley Cup Finals.

professional—relating to a player or team that makes money playing a sport

save—when a goalie stops a shot on the goal from scoring

wild card—a team selected to fill in the final spots of a playoff tournament

TO LEARN MORE

AT THE LIBRARY

Hoena, Blake. *The Science of Hockey with Max Axiom, Super Scientist.* North Mankato, Minn.: Capstone Press, 2016.

Morey, Allan. *Hockey Records.* Minneapolis, Minn.: Bellwether Media, 2018.

Omoth, Tyler. *Pro Hockey's Championship.* North Mankato, Minn.: Capstone Press, 2018.

ON THE WEB

Learning more about the Stanley Cup Finals is as easy as 1, 2, 3.

1. Go to www.factsurfer.com.

2. Enter "Stanley Cup Finals" into the search box.

3. Click the "Surf" button and you will see a list of related web sites.

With factsurfer.com, finding more information is just a click away.

INDEX

The images in this book are reproduced through the courtesy of: Dom Gagne/Cal Sport Media/ Newscom, front cover (athlete); meunierd, front cover (trophy), p. 9; Dave Sandrod/ NHLI/ Getty, p. 4; Justin K. Aller/NHLI/ Getty, p. 5; Debora Robinson/NHLI/ Getty, pp. 6-7; Frederick Breedon/ Getty, pp. 8-9; Bruce Bennett Studios/ Getty, pp. 10, 11; Hockey Hall of Fame and Museum/ Wikipedia, p. 12; Charles Hoff/NY Daily News/ Getty, p. 13; Cal Sport Meida/ Alamy, pp. 14-15; Joe Sargent/NHLI/ Getty, pp. 16-17; Jeff Vinnick/NHLI/ Getty, p. 20; Ryan Remiorz/ AP Images, p. 21.